Dr. Olivia Sanders

ASK DR. LIBBY

ABC

Illustrated by Don Howard

ISBN-13: 978-1-945019-00-5

ISBN-10: 1-945019-00-X

Quintessential Publishing

www.quintessential.pub

info@quintessential.pub

Special discounts are available on quantity purchases by corporations, associations, and others. For details, contact the publisher at the address above.

A is for Apple

SO ROSY AND RED

B IS FOR BUNNY

AND ALSO FOR BED

C IS FOR CAT

AND ALSO FOR COW

D

IS FOR DOG

BOW WOW!

THAT SAYS BOW WOW

E

IS FOR ELEPHANT

WE SEE AT THE ZOO

F IS FOR FLOWERS

PINK, WHITE AND BLUE

G IS FOR GIRAFFE

WHOSE NECK IS SO LONG, AND
ALSO FOR GIANT, SO BIG AND SO STRONG

H

IS FOR HOUSE

THERE ARE TEN ON MY STREET

I IS FOR ICE CREAM

SO COLD AND SO SWEET

J IS FOR JACKET

WE WEAR WHEN IT'S COLD
MY FAVORITE ONE IS BLUE AND GOLD

K

IS FOR KITE

WE FLY TO THE SKY

L IS FOR LAMB

WHO KICKS HIS HEELS HIGH

M IS FOR MILK

WE DRINK A GLASS EVERYDAY

N IS FOR NEEDLE

WE CAN'T FIND IN THE HAY

O IS FOR ORANGE

THAT WE LOVE TO EAT

P IS FOR PIG

WITH FUNNY LITTLE FEET

Q IS FOR QUILT

WE PUT ON OUR BEDS
BEFORE WE REST OUR SLEEPY HEADS

R IS FOR RABBIT

AND ALSO FOR RAT
BOTH ARE AFRAID OF A LITTLE OLD CAT

S IS FOR STARS WE SEE
IN THE SKY

ALSO FOR SALLY WHO IS VERY SHY

T IS FOR TRAVEL

BY BUS, CAR OR TRAIN

U IS FOR UMBRELLA

WE CARRY IN THE RAIN

V IS FOR VICTORY

WHEN WE WIN THE GAME

W IS FOR WAGON

LET'S TAKE A RIDE

X IS FOR X-RAY

TO SEE ON EACH SIDE

Y IS FOR YELLOW

THE COLOR OF THE MOON

Z IS FOR THE WORDS: ZIP, ZAP AND ZOOM!

AND NOW THAT OUR ABCs HAVE
COME TO AN END,

I HOPE YOU HAVE ENJOYED THEM,
WITH MUCH LOVE I SEND.

DR. LiBBY

ABOUT THE AUTHOR

Dr. Olivia Harris Sanders was a distinguished educator within the state of Alabama. Working in the field of education for more than 50 years, Dr. Sanders' professional experience spanned from elementary to collegiate classrooms. As a professional in education, she served as an educational and accreditation consultant for In-Service Education for the following schools systems: Madison County, Huntsville City, Morgan County, Decatur City and Guntersville City. In recognition for her dedication to education and determination to improve teaching learning strategies, she received countless awards, honors and citations from professional, civic, and community organizations, colleagues, and students.

Dr. Olivia Harris Sanders was born and reared in Birmingham, Alabama. Nicknamed Libby, she received the Bachelor of Education degree from Miles College. Further studies earned her the Master of Science degree and AA Certificate in School Administration and Supervision from Alabama A&M University and the Doctor of Education degree from the University of Alabama-Tuscaloosa in Curriculum Development and Supervision. Dr. Sanders began working on the Dr. Libby © series in 2012 while homeschooling her youngest grandson, Will. She completed three titles which include: 'Ask Dr. Libby: ABCs', "Will Visits The Big City: New York", and "Dr. Libby's Fun and Activities". As a testament to her legacy in education, her family has continued her work through the creation of the Dr. Libby Children's Series.